He needs to justify ch[...]

Don't cater to smal[...]
them power.

Jake needs to acknowlege it to gym

video of the gym ewner. Subtext needs to be
clear. Less than 4 minutes, Explain why Jake is there.
Explain why I'm stepping back. Jake admits how

Unless otherwise indicated, all Scripture quotations are taken from the Amplified Bible (AMP). Scripture quotations
taken from the Amplified® Bible. Copyright © 1954, 1958, 1962, 1964, 1965, 1987 by The Lockman Foundation. Used by
permission. (www.lockman.org)

Scripture quotations marked "NIV" are taken from THE HOLY BIBLE, NEW INTERNATIONAL VERSION®, NIV®
Copyright © 1973, 1973, 1984, 2011 by Biblica, Inc.® Used by permission. All rights reserved worldwide.

Scripture quotations marked "NKJV" are taken from the New King James Version. Scripture taken from the New King
James Version. Copyright © 1982 by Thomas Nelson, Inc. Used by permission. All rights reserved.

things are going to change. No gossip in the bud

contents

introduction	4
loved by God	8
saved	16
valued & precious in His sight	22
knowing who you are in Christ	26
abiding in relationship with God	30
strengthened & equipped	34
filled with hope	38
at rest in your soul	44
experiencing new beginnings	50

God loves you! Those are the three most powerful words I could ever tell you. And living in the truth of that promise is what will free you to experience the joy-filled, overcoming, abundant life Jesus died to give you.

Jeremiah 31:3 says, . . . *I have loved you with an everlasting love; therefore with loving-kindness have I drawn you and continued My faithfulness to you.*

An "everlasting love" means God loved you before you ever

knew Him (Jeremiah 1:5); He loves you even when you make mistakes (Romans 5:8); He loves you today (2 Corinthians 6:2); and He promises to love you forever (Psalm 23:6).

The key to receiving and living in God's love is to learn what He says about you in His Word and believe His promises are true. As you study the Scriptures, you'll see that God is not distant or angry — He is close to you, and He wants to live in a personal relationship with you each and every day.

I pray that the scriptures in this book will encourage you deeply. As you meditate on each promise and begin applying it to your life, I believe you'll discover that God's love affects every area of your life.

Enjoy this life-changing journey. And never forget . . .
YOU ARE LOVED.

Joyce Meyer

Yet amid all these things we are more than conquerors and gain a surpassing victory through Him Who loved us.

ROMANS 8:37

For I am persuaded beyond doubt (am sure) that neither death nor life, nor angels nor principalities, nor things impending and threatening nor things to come, nor powers, nor height nor depth, nor anything else in all creation will be able to separate us from the love of God which is in Christ Jesus our Lord.

ROMANS 8:38-39

For God so greatly loved and dearly prized the world that He [even] gave up His only begotten (unique) Son, so that whoever believes in (trusts in, clings to, relies on) Him shall not perish (come to destruction, be lost) but have eternal (everlasting) life.

JOHN 3:16

In this the love of God was made manifest (displayed) where we are concerned: in that God sent His Son, the only begotten or unique [Son], into the world so that we might live through Him.

1 JOHN 4:9

But God shows and clearly proves His [own] love for us by the fact that while we were still sinners, Christ (the Messiah, the Anointed One) died for us.

ROMANS 5:8

Your love, Lord, reaches to the heavens, your faithfulness to the skies.

PSALM 36:5 NIV

. . . I pray that you, being rooted and established in love, may have power, together with all the Lord's holy people, to grasp how wide and long and high and deep is the love of Christ, and to know this love that surpasses knowledge—that you may be filled to the measure of all the fullness of God.

EPHESIANS 3:17-19 NIV

For it is by free grace (God's unmerited favor) that you are saved (delivered from judgment and made partakers of Christ's salvation) through [your] faith. And this [salvation] is not of yourselves [of your own doing, it came not through your own striving], but it is the gift of God.

EPHESIANS 2:8

Even when we were dead (slain) by [our own] shortcomings and trespasses, He made us alive together in fellowship and in union with Christ; [He gave us the very life of Christ Himself, the same new life with which He quickened Him, for] it is by grace (His favor and mercy which you did not deserve) that you are saved (delivered from judgment and made partakers of Christ's salvation).

EPHESIANS 2:5

[The Father] has delivered and drawn us to Himself out of the control and the dominion of darkness and has transferred us into the kingdom of the Son of His love, in Whom we have our redemption through His blood, [which means] the forgiveness of our sins.

COLOSSIANS 1:13-14

For God so greatly loved and dearly prized the world that He [even] gave up His only begotten (unique) Son, so that whoever believes in (trusts in, clings to, relies on) Him shall not perish (come to destruction, be lost) but have eternal (everlasting) life.

JOHN 3:16

If you declare with your mouth, "Jesus is Lord," and believe in your heart that God raised him from the dead, you will be saved. For it is with your heart that you believe and are justified, and it is with your mouth that you profess your faith and are saved.

ROMANS 10:9-10 NIV

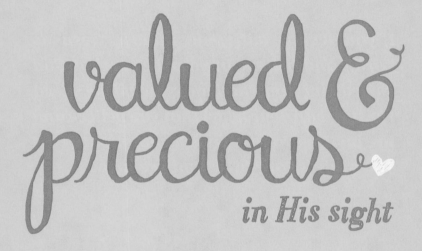

But [even] the very hairs of your head are all numbered. Do not be struck with fear or seized with alarm; you are of greater worth than many [flocks] of sparrows.

LUKE 12:7

I praise you because I am fearfully and wonderfully made; your works are wonderful, I know that full well.

PSALM 139:14 NIV

. . . [In His love] He chose us [actually picked us out for Himself as His own] in Christ before the foundation of the world. . . .

EPHESIANS 1:4

knowing who you are

in Christ

And the Lord shall make you the head, and not the tail; and you shall be above only, and you shall not be beneath, if you heed the commandments of the Lord your God which I command you this day and are watchful to do them.

DEUTERONOMY 28:13

27

Now if we are children, then we are heirs—heirs of God and co-heirs with Christ, if indeed we share in his sufferings in order that we may also share in his glory.

ROMANS 8:17 NIV

You are the light of the world. A city set on a hill cannot be hidden.

MATTHEW 5:14

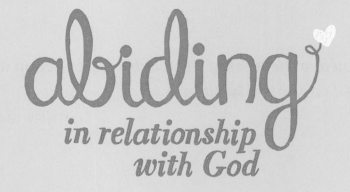

And we know (understand, recognize, are conscious of, by observation and by experience) and believe (adhere to and put faith in and rely on) the love God cherishes for us. God is love, and he who dwells and continues in love dwells and continues in God, and God dwells and continues in him.

1 JOHN 4:16

The Lord appeared to us in the past, saying:
"I have loved you with an everlasting love; I
have drawn you with unfailing kindness."

JEREMIAH 31:3 NIV

I have loved you, [just] as the Father has loved Me; abide in My love [continue in His love with Me].

In the day when I called, You answered me; and You strengthened me with strength (might and inflexibility to temptation) in my inner self.

35

. . . Be strong in the Lord [be empowered through your union with Him]; draw your strength from Him [that strength which His boundless might provides].

EPHESIANS 6:10

His intention was the perfecting and the full equipping of the saints (His consecrated people), [that they should do] the work of ministering toward building up Christ's body (the church).

EPHESIANS 4:12

May the God of your hope so fill you with all joy and peace in believing [through the experience of your faith] that by the power of the Holy Spirit you may abound and be overflowing (bubbling over) with hope.

ROMANS 15:13

You are my hiding place and my shield; I hope in Your word.

PSALM 119:114

And now, Lord, what do I wait for and expect?
My hope and expectation are in You.

PSALM 39:7

For surely there is a latter end [a future and a reward], and your hope and expectation shall not be cut off.

PROVERBS 23:18

*But if we hope for what is still **unseen by us**,*
we wait for it with patience and composure.

ROMANS 8:25

at rest

in your soul

Come to Me, all you who labor and are heavy-laden and overburdened, and I will cause you to rest. [I will ease and relieve and refresh your souls.]

MATTHEW 11:28

Casting the whole of your care [all your anx-ieties, all your worries, all your concerns, once and for all] on Him, for He cares for you affectionately and cares about you watchfully.

There remains, then, a Sabbath-rest for the people of God; for anyone who enters God's rest also rests from their works, just as God did from his.

HEBREWS 4:9-10 NIV

Let be and be still, and know (recognize and understand) that I am God. I will be exalted among the nations! I will be exalted in the earth!

He who dwells in the secret place of the Most High shall remain stable and fixed under the shadow of the Almighty [Whose power no foe can withstand].

PSALM 91:1

Therefore if any person is [ingrafted] in Christ (the Messiah) he is a new creation (a new creature altogether); the old [previous moral and spiritual condition] has passed away. Behold, the fresh and new has come!

2 CORINTHIANS 5:17

. . . One thing I do [it is my one aspiration]: forgetting what lies behind and straining forward to what lies ahead, I press on toward the goal to win the [supreme and heavenly] prize to which God in Christ Jesus is calling us upward.

PHILIPPIANS 3:13-14

Behold, I am doing a new thing! Now it springs forth; do you not perceive and know it and will you not give heed to it? I will even make a way in the wilderness and rivers in the desert.

ISAIAH 43:19

Because of the Lord's great love we are not consumed, for his compassions never fail. They are new every morning; great is your faithfulness.

LAMENTATIONS 3:22-23 NIV

But those who wait for the Lord [who expect, look for, and hope in Him] shall change and renew their strength and power; they shall lift their wings and mount up [close to God] as eagles [mount up to the sun]; they shall run and not be weary, they shall walk and not faint or become tired.

ISAIAH 40:31

Loving *others*

I give you a new commandment: that you should love one another. Just as I have loved you, so you too should love one another.

JOHN 13:34

Beloved, if God loved us so [very much],
we also ought to love one another.

1 JOHN 4:11

Beloved, let us love one another, for love is (springs) from God; and he who loves [his fellowmen] is begotten (born) of God and is coming [progressively] to know and understand God [to perceive and recognize and get a better and clearer knowledge of Him].

1 JOHN 4:7

For his anger lasts only a moment, but his favor lasts a lifetime; weeping may stay for the night, but rejoicing comes in the morning.

PSALM 30:5 NIV

For You, Lord, will bless the [uncompromisingly] righteous [him who is upright and in right standing with You]; as with a shield You will surround him with goodwill (pleasure and favor).

PSALM 5:12

For the Lord God is a Sun and Shield; the Lord bestows [present] grace and favor and [future] glory (honor, splendor, and heavenly bliss)! No good thing will He withhold from those who walk uprightly.

PSALM 84:11

And become useful and helpful and kind to one another, tenderhearted (compassionate, understanding, loving-hearted), forgiving one another [readily and freely], as God in Christ forgave you.

EPHESIANS 4:32

If we [freely] admit that we have sinned and confess our sins, He is faithful and just (true to His own nature and promises) and will forgive our sins [dismiss our lawlessness] and [continuously] cleanse us from all unrighteousness [everything not in conformity to His will in purpose, thought, and action].

1 JOHN 1:9

For this is My blood of the new covenant, which [ratifies the agreement and] is being poured out for many for the forgiveness of sins.

MATTHEW 26:28

trusting
in God

[Most] blessed is the man who believes in, trusts in, and relies on the Lord, and whose hope and confidence the Lord is.

JEREMIAH 17:7

Lean on, trust in, and be confident in the Lord with all your heart and mind and do not rely on your own insight or understanding.

PROVERBS 3:5

Delight yourself also in the Lord, and He will give you the desires and secret petitions of your heart. Commit your way to the Lord [roll and repose each care of your load on Him]; trust (lean on, rely on, and be confident) also in Him and He will bring it to pass.

PSALM 37:4-5

I will say of the Lord, He is my Refuge and my Fortress, my God; on Him I lean and rely, and in Him I [confidently] trust!

PSALM 91:2

Jesus said, . . . Blessed and happy and to be envied are those who have never seen Me and yet have believed and adhered to and trusted and relied on Me.

For our sake He made Christ [virtually] to be sin Who knew no sin, so that in and through Him we might become [endued with, viewed as being in, and examples of] the righteousness of God [what we ought to be, approved and acceptable and in right relationship with Him, by His goodness].

Accept one another, then, just as Christ accepted you, in order to bring praise to God.

ROMANS 15:7 NIV

. . . He chose us in Him before the foundation of the world, that we should be holy and without blame before Him in love, having predestined us to adoption as sons by Jesus Christ to Himself, according to the good pleasure of His will, to the praise of the glory of His grace, by which He made us accepted in the Beloved.

EPHESIANS 1:4-6 NKJV

That He might present the church to Himself in glorious splendor, without spot or wrinkle or any such things [that she might be holy and faultless].

EPHESIANS 5:27

Therefore, [there is] now no condemnation (no adjudging guilty of wrong) for those who are in Christ Jesus, who live [and] walk not after the dictates of the flesh, but after the dictates of the Spirit.

ROMANS 8:1

enjoying
everyday life

Rejoice in the Lord always [delight, gladden yourselves in Him]; again I say, Rejoice!

PHILIPPIANS 4:4

The thief comes only in order to steal and kill and destroy. I came that they may have and enjoy life, and have it in abundance (to the full, till it overflows).

JOHN 10:10

Without having seen Him, you love Him;
though you do not [even] now see Him, you
believe in Him and exult and thrill with
inexpressible and glorious (triumphant,
heavenly) joy.

1 PETER 1:8

[After all] the kingdom of God is not a matter of [getting the] food and drink [one likes], but instead it is righteousness (that state which makes a person acceptable to God) and [heart] peace and joy in the Holy Spirit.

ROMANS 14:17

A happy heart is good medicine and a cheerful mind works healing, but a broken spirit dries up the bones.

PROVERBS 17:22

Be strong, courageous, and firm; fear not nor be in terror before them, for it is the Lord your God Who goes with you; He will not fail you or forsake you.

DEUTERONOMY 31:6

. . . Behold, I am with you all the days (perpetually, uniformly, and on every occasion), to the [very] close and consummation of the age. Amen (so let it be).

MATTHEW 28:20

And the Lord said, My Presence shall go with you, and I will give you rest.

EXODUS 33:14

I have strength for all things in Christ Who empowers me [I am ready for anything and equal to anything through Him Who infuses inner strength into me; I am self-sufficient in Christ's sufficiency].

PHILIPPIANS 4:13

. . . Be strong, vigorous, and very courageous.
Be not afraid, neither be dismayed, for the
Lord your God is with you wherever you go.

JOSHUA 1:9

Fear not [there is nothing to fear], for I am with you; do not look around you in terror and be dismayed, for I am your God. I will strengthen and harden you to difficulties, yes, I will help you; yes, I will hold you up and retain you with My [victorious] right hand of rightness and justice.

ISAIAH 41:10

There is no fear in love [dread does not exist], but full-grown (complete, perfect) love turns fear out of doors and expels every trace of terror! . . .

1 JOHN 4:18

For God did not give us a spirit of timidity (of cowardice, of craven and cringing and fawning fear), but [He has given us a spirit] of power and of love and of calm and well-balanced mind and discipline and self-control.

2 TIMOTHY 1:7

Do not fret or have any anxiety about anything, but in every circumstance and in everything, by prayer and petition (definite requests), with thanksgiving, continue to make your wants known to God.

PHILIPPIANS 4:6

But Jesus said to them, It is I; be not afraid!
[I AM; stop being frightened!]

submitting to God's

wisdom & correction

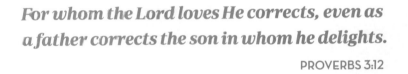

For whom the Lord loves He corrects, even as a father corrects the son in whom he delights.

PROVERBS 3:12

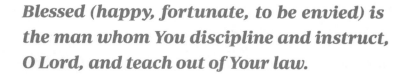

Blessed (happy, fortunate, to be envied) is the man whom You discipline and instruct, O Lord, and teach out of Your law.

PSALM 94:12

Those whom I [dearly and tenderly] love, I tell their faults and convict and convince and reprove and chasten [I discipline and instruct them]. So be enthusiastic and in earnest and burning with zeal and repent [changing your mind and attitude].

REVELATION 3:19

. . . Because of our faith in Him, we dare to have the boldness (courage and confidence) of free access (an unreserved approach to God with freedom and without fear).

Let us then fearlessly and confidently and boldly draw near to the throne of grace (the throne of God's unmerited favor to us sinners), that we may receive mercy [for our failures] and find grace to help in good time for every need [appropriate help and well-timed help, coming just when we need it].

HEBREWS 4:16

Not that we are fit (qualified and sufficient in ability) of ourselves to form personal judgments or to claim or count anything as coming from us, but our power and ability and sufficiency are from God.

2 CORINTHIANS 3:5

For the Lord shall be your confidence, firm and strong, and shall keep your foot from being caught [in a trap or some hidden danger].

PROVERBS 3:26

So we take comfort and are encouraged and confidently and boldly say, The Lord is my Helper; I will not be seized with alarm [I will not fear or dread or be terrified]. What can man do to me?

HEBREWS 13:6

righteous

in Christ

[All] are justified and made upright and in right standing with God, freely and gratuitously by His grace (His unmerited favor and mercy), through the redemption which is [provided] in Christ Jesus.

ROMANS 3:24

And He raised us up together with Him and made us sit down together [giving us joint seating with Him] in the heavenly sphere [by virtue of our being] in Christ Jesus (the Messiah, the Anointed One).

EPHESIANS 2:6

It is because of him that you are in Christ Jesus, who has become for us wisdom from God—that is, our righteousness, holiness and redemption.

1 CORINTHIANS 1:30 NIV

Yet now has [Christ, the Messiah] reconciled [you to God] in the body of His flesh through death, in order to present you holy and faultless and irreproachable in His [the Father's] presence.

COLOSSIANS 1:22

Christ is the culmination of the law so that there may be righteousness for everyone who believes.

ROMANS 10:4 NIV

And my God will liberally supply (fill to the full) your every need according to His riches in glory in Christ Jesus.

PHILIPPIANS 4:19

I have been young and now am old, yet have I not seen the [uncompromisingly] righteous forsaken or their seed begging bread.

PSALM 37:25

So Abraham called the name of that place The Lord Will Provide. And it is said to this day, On the mount of the Lord it will be provided.

GENESIS 22:14

And [God] Who provides seed for the sower and bread for eating will also provide and multiply your [resources for] sowing and increase the fruits of your righteousness [which manifests itself in active goodness, kindness, and charity].

2 CORINTHIANS 9:10

The Lord is my Shepherd [to feed, guide, and shield me], I shall not lack.

PSALM 23:1

For the vision is yet for an appointed time and it hastens to the end [fulfillment]; it will not deceive or disappoint. Though it tarry, wait [earnestly] for it, because it will surely come; it will not be behindhand on its appointed day.

HABAKKUK 2:3

The Lord will perfect that which concerns me; Your mercy and loving-kindness, O Lord, endure forever—forsake not the works of Your own hands.

PSALM 138:8

We are assured and know that [God being a partner in their labor] all things work together and are [fitting into a plan] for good to and for those who love God and are called according to [His] design and purpose.

ROMANS 8:28

. . . God has not rejected and disowned His people [whose destiny] He had marked out and appointed and foreknown from the beginning . . .

ROMANS 11:2

Who has prepared and done this, calling forth and guiding the destinies of the generations [of the nations] from the beginning? I, the Lord—the first [existing before history began] and with the last [an ever-present, unchanging God]—I am He.

ISAIAH 41:4

believing

God can do anything

For with God nothing is ever impossible and no word from God shall be without power or impossible of fulfillment.

LUKE 1:37

But Jesus looked at them and said, With men this is impossible, but all things are possible with God.

MATTHEW 19:26

And I will do [I Myself will grant] whatever you ask in My Name [as presenting all that I AM], so that the Father may be glorified and extolled in (through) the Son.

JOHN 14:13

living in God's

grace

For out of His fullness (abundance) we have all received [all had a share and we were all supplied with] one grace after another and spiritual blessing upon spiritual blessing and even favor upon favor and gift [heaped] upon gift.

JOHN 1:16

And God is able to make all grace (every favor and earthly blessing) come to you in abundance, so that you may always and under all circumstances and whatever the need be self-sufficient [possessing enough to require no aid or support and furnished in abundance for every good work and charitable donation].

2 CORINTHIANS 9:8

But he said to me, "My grace is sufficient for you, for my power is made perfect in weakness." Therefore I will boast all the more gladly about my weaknesses, so that Christ's power may rest on me.

2 CORINTHIANS 12:9 NIV

For sin shall not [any longer] exert dominion over you, since now you are not under Law [as slaves], but under grace [as subjects of God's favor and mercy].

ROMANS 6:14

For while the Law was given through Moses, grace (unearned, undeserved favor and spiritual blessing) and truth came through Jesus Christ.

JOHN 1:17

JOYCE MEYER MINISTRIES
Sharing Christ - Loving People

Joyce Meyer Ministries is called to share the Gospel and extend the love of Christ. Through media we teach people how to apply biblical truth to every aspect of their lives and encourage God's people to serve the world around them. Through our missions arm, *Hand of Hope*, we provide global humanitarian aid, feed the hungry, clothe the poor, minister to the elderly, widows and orphans, visit prisoners and reach out to people of all ages and in all walks of life. *Joyce Meyer Ministries* is built on a foundation of faith, integrity and dedicated supporters who share this call.

For more information about *Joyce Meyer Ministries*, please visit joycemeyer.org or call (800) 727-9673. Outside the U.S. call (636) 349-0303.

Joyce Meyer Ministries • P.O. Box 655 • Fenton, MO 63026 USA • joycemeyer.org

 facebook.com/**joycemeyerministries**   @joycemeyer